TO Tiffani Take act[illegible] On you[illegible] & Dre[illegible] Pull th[illegible]

MW01008766

Pull the Darn Trigger

7 Winning Strategies to Achieving Your Goals

Una Richards
www.pullthedarntrigger.com

Pull the Darn Trigger
7 Winning Strategies to Achieving Your Goals
www.pullthedarntrigger.com

Copyright © 2016 by Una Richards

All rights reserved. No portion of this book may be reproduced mechanically, electronically, or by any other means, including photocopying, without permission of the publisher or author except in the case of brief quotations embodied in critical articles and reviews. It is illegal to copy this book, post it to a website, or distribute it by any other means without permission from the publisher or author.

Limits of Liability and Disclaimer of Warranty
The author and publisher shall not be liable for your misuse of this material. This book is strictly for informational and educational purposes.

Warning – Disclaimer
The purpose of this book is to educate and entertain. The author and/or publisher do not guarantee that anyone following these techniques, suggestions, tips, ideas, or strategies will become successful. The author and/or publisher shall have neither liability nor responsibility to anyone with respect to any loss or damage caused, or alleged to be caused, directly or indirectly by the information contained in this book.

Publisher
10-10-10 Publishing
Markham, ON   Canada

Printed in the United States of America
ISBN: 978-1542614498

Contents

Dedication

I dedicate this book to those individuals who have a dream, and want so much to realize it, but don't know where to start, or may be too afraid to follow through. I say to you, "You can do it." Don't deny yourself the opportunity to achieve success. If you can dream it, then you are able to actualize it; so, "Go for it."

Acknowledgements

I acknowledge my mother Maudlin Mason, who has always believed in me and encouraged me to pursue my dreams. She always told me that I could do anything I put my mind to. She also told me to put God first in all that I do, and He will direct my path. One of her infamous lines is "In all your doing, get wisdom."

To my son, Jason, and daughter, Sophia, for making me proud and for being the best two children I could ever hope for.

To the New Peaks organization, founded by T. Harv Eker, author of *Secrets of a Millionaire Mind*, and current CEO, Adam Markel, for their teaching and developing techniques, and for helping me to strive to reach new peaks.

Testimonials

In her book *Pull the Darn Trigger*, Una uses a practical approach to help individual identify barriers or obstacles getting in the way of them achieving their goals. She pinpointed some simple yet relatable stumbling blocks such as fear, self-doubt and or lack of self-confidence that could be holding some individuals back and therefore sabotaging their efforts. Her pragmatic approach, if applied, could transform individual's lives by helping them to overcome these obstacles and discover their true potential with profound results. Reading this book is truly inspiring.
Tasha Mosley, Solicitor General of Clayton County

Pull the Darn Trigger is such an appropriate title of Una's book. She is an inspiring leader who motivates her staff to continuously grow to develop their skills. She encourages her team to work to improve their personal growth while providing quality service every time to every customer. Since joining our team she has raised the bar and has improved our service levels to a higher standard.
Jonna Kirkwood, COO, Georgia Region, Kaiser Permanente

Foreword

Pull the Darn Trigger is a practical, no-nonsense guide that will appeal to you, if you have a dream or a desire to achieve a goal, but for one reason or another you are having a difficult time doing so.

If you feel stuck and you have put your goal or dream on hold, this book will motivate and inspire you to step out, and encourage you to move forward and pursue it.

Una challenges you to take the limits off yourself and act in spite of any fear or self-doubt. She has introduced some techniques to help you navigate your way successfully to achieve those goals.

She also challenges you to step out of your comfort zone by identifying and confronting some of those self-limiting beliefs, as well as external factors that may be holding you back from taking action, such as fear of failure, lack of self-confidence, procrastination and other distractions.

I highly recommend this book!

Raymond Aaron
New York Times Bestselling Author

Introduction

The purpose of this book is to encourage and inspire those struggling to get past some of the issues that may be holding them back from achieving their goals. There are times when an individual knows what they want to do, but for various reasons, they may struggle to get moving and implement it. Sometimes they may be aware, or unaware, of that thing that is holding them back. In other words, they are having difficulty pulling that trigger. Even if they have done the preliminary work and have completed the prerequisites, they have just come to a cross road and stay stuck.

I can definitely identify with those scenarios. As a result of that same struggle, I started to do a self-analysis of the time and the thousands of dollars that I've invested in my education, self-developmental courses, coaching, conferences, seminars, and webinars—the list goes on and on. I realize that I'm not doing the things that I promised myself I would do, within the timeframe I had committed to doing them. It's not because I lacked the time, resources, or support; I had all that I needed to get started, but didn't. So, to put myself at ease, I'd take another course, and I tell myself that I would be ready by the time the other course was completed. Each time that I stalled, I spent more money, but hardly learned anything new. Why? I already had all the information I needed to get started and to move forward. In other words, I was afraid to pull the darn trigger. I realized that the only thing that was holding me back was me. I needed to get out of my own way and stop blocking my success, which was preventing me from reaching my desired goals. For over two and a half years, I attended daily or weekly classes, online workshops, and coaching sessions, and had not begun practicing stock options trading as I had declared to myself that I would, two years earlier.

To make my pain even worse, I ran into a student, from one of my previous online coaching classes, and asked how he was doing with his stock options trading. He stated that he was doing very well. I probed further as to what exactly he was doing, and he stated that he was using the same concepts taught in class, as well as the advanced sessions we both paid extra for, so we could excel. I seriously started to question myself as to why I was not doing the same. In fact, I had more exposure to options trading because I had been taking courses prior to the current class we attended. I have come to realize that I was subconsciously sabotaging myself. So, whatever your reason is for not taking action to achieve your goal, I challenge you to start today. *Pull the darn trigger* on that goal you've been wanting to achieve.

Chapter 1

Have a Clear Goal

- What is your goal?
- Why do you want the goal?
- What steps are you willing to take to get to the goal?

What is your goal? Your goal needs to be specific enough that you can articulate it when asked. If your goal is not clear, you will have difficulty in acquiring the right resources, information, or assistance, in order to achieve it.

Why do you want this goal? If you start with your *"why,"* it will be the driving force to accomplishing your goal. Keep it in the front of your mind. What will it do for you? In other words, what will be the end result after you have achieved your goal? The first step after identifying your goal is to write it down. There is a saying: *"A goal is not a goal if it is not written; it is only a wish."* If you have a desire to accomplish a goal, or you have a dream that you wish to fulfill, and it is only in your head, more likely than not, it will not be actualized. You think you will successfully achieve it; however, it is said that people often fail because they have no structure or clear direction for achieving their goals.

You need to lay out clear directions of where you want to go and what happens when you get there. Consequently, your written goal needs to be clear and focused. Just as it is easier to get where you are going faster with a GPS or a road map, so are your goals easier to navigate if you have clear directions. Have a blueprint—a plan of what you intend to accomplish. Steven Covey, author of the book, *Seven Habits of Highly Successful People,* said to develop a personal mission statement. Your mission statement makes you the leader of your life; you create your own destiny and secure the future that you envision. He said, that to accomplish or achieve what you intend, the first step is to write it down. When you write down your goals, you are making an agreement with yourself. You are committing to doing your part to fulfill this agreement. Writing down your goals helps you to clarify the vision that you have in your mind and keeps you focused. Writing down your goals also motivates you to take action. Having a written goal increases the odds of accomplishing it. There have been numerous studies done, indicating that people who write down their goals, achieve them at a much higher rate than people who do not. Results don't lie; so, follow-through and write it down. Next, your goal must be specific. Clarify what you expect to achieve by accomplishing the goal, and why.

Be sure that it is not just a fleeting thought, or a "would be nice to have," just to appease your love ones or to impress others. Access the real reasons why you want this goal, and if it truly is your desire, then go for it.

Make a list of the most important things that you must get done, and commit to doing them by making them a priority. Be clear about what you need to be doing, and place a timeline on when you need to have it done. If you don't, your mind will be distracted, and your focus will be on non-essential tasks, instead of on your main overall goal.

To help you achieve your goals, there are several success formulas. One of the most popular success formula is the Smart (S.M.A.R.T.) goal formula.

- S stands for specific – the goal should be specific and be able to identify *who, what, when, where,* and *why.* It should be tangible.
- M stands for measurable – the goal should be measurable; you should be able to track your progress and accomplishment.
- A stands for attainable – how do you plan to achieve your goal?
- R stands for relevance – is it worthwhile having?
- T stands for timely – when do you plan to achieve it? What is your time frame? It must be specific; you must have a specific deadline.

Once you have completed the process of writing your goal, display it. Post your goal in an area in plain sight. Seeing is believing. Seeing it every day helps you to stay focused, and reminds you of what you need to do. Read it out aloud. By doing so, your subconscious mind will believe it and go to work to help you achieve it. Your subconscious doesn't know the difference between true or false. It will not pause to reason or wonder; it only follows whatever instructions you give it. That's why it is imperative to think and stay positive, no matter what. This is one of those situations where you get out what you put in. If you plant positive thoughts of success and achievement daily, you will reap the benefits later, even when things are not working as planned. So, read your goals out loud to cement them in your subconscious mind.

After you have written it down and posted it, the next step is to organize it. You want to develop a plan to achieve it. Your *why* will be the driving force that will motivate and propel you to the next level. Shoot for the moon—if you miss, you'll still be in the stars. Your *why* needs to be so big, and so audacious that when you think about achieving this goal, it should ignite you so that you burst with feelings of enthusiasm. It should motivate you to the point where you can see your life, and the lives of those around you, changing for the better as a result of it. So, think *big*, think positive, and see yourself accomplishing your goals. Dare to dream;

when you dream *big*, whatever you focus on, expands, and when it does, your mind will go to work to achieve and make it happen. Remember, your mind does not know the difference; it will do whatever you tell it. So, write it down, and make it plain. Develop and recite your affirmation, it will generate a certain amount of energy around you. When it seems that you are off track, or everything around you is falling apart, it will be your GPS to redirect you, keep you focused, and re-energize you. In your daily affirmation, repeat words, such as, "I have," or "I am." Speak in the present tense as if it's already done, and you have already reached your goal. *"...call those things which be not as though they were."* – Romans 4:17 (KJV). As you speak of your goal, it builds self-confidence and gets you closer to *pulling the trigger* to make it happen.

Your goal should be so embedded in your subconscious mind that if someone were to awaken you in the middle of the night from a deep sleep and ask what your goal is, you could tell them, and go back to dreaming. That's when you know you are passionate, and you are on a mission to getting what you want.

What's Holding You Back?

So, you have a clear goal, you have written it down, and you have posted it. You have invested your time and your money. You are also affirming what you want to manifest, but you are not making the type of progress you thought you would have made by now, therefore, you are questioning yourself. What's holding you back?

Have you ever truly desired to do something but find yourself holding back, or taking yourself out, as you get closer to achieving it? What's stopping you? What are others telling you? More importantly, what are you telling yourself? What's getting in the way of the accomplishment of your goals? Another question you need to ask yourself is whether this thing, or person, that you think is holding you back, is worth it. If the answer is a resounding *no*, then take a step and start heading towards your goal. What is it costing you as a result of not moving forward? Is it costing additional irretrievable time and money? The longer it takes you to act on the commitment that you made to yourself the longer it will take you to see the result. So many people are destined for greatness, but, because of perceived obstacles and barriers, they allow things to get in their way, so they feel stuck, and, therefore, they do nothing. This type of behavior is labeled in psychology as *learned helplessness*—a feeling that you can't overcome certain obstacles placed in your path, so you give up trying, even after the obstacle has been long removed. Many times, it could have been something from the past that no longer exists; but because it was once a problem, even though it doesn't exist anymore, it continues to be a barrier that stands in the way of your progress. The *learned helplessness* theory has been studied using animals such as elephants, dogs, rats, etc., in order to change their behaviors and to study the effect of depression and stress. One example points to the training of elephants, starting at a young age.

"When elephant trainers in India catch a baby elephant, they tie one of its legs to a post with a rope. The baby elephant struggles and struggles but it can't get free. For days, the elephant pulls and strains at the rope. Gradually, it learns that struggle is useless and it gives up.

When the elephant grows up, the trainer keeps it tied to the same rope, in the same way. And, even though it can now break the rope and get away, it stands passively and waits for the trainer to come and get it. It has developed what is called 'learned helplessness.' It has learned that the struggle is useless. As a result of repeated failure experiences earlier in life, the elephant has learned a self-imposed limitation."

– Learned helplessness: How to tame a baby elephant... Posted by Wayne under Life, Success Tags: Life, Success. Told by Bryan Tracy

Learned helplessness, in psychology, means "a mental state in which an organism forced to bear aversive stimuli that are painful or otherwise unpleasant, becomes unable or unwilling to avoid subsequent encounters with those stimuli, even if they are *escapable,* presumably because it has learned that it cannot control the situation." Encyclopedia Britannica. If you allow self-doubt and negative self-talk to dominate your thoughts and prevent you from pursuing your goal, then seek counseling to help identify and overcome it. You may feel beaten down from criticism or discouragement from others, or you may not understand what is blocking you. Seek help so that you can move forward. Remind yourself that you are resourceful, you are a victor and an overcomer.

Regardless of the lack of support or enthusiasm by others around you, press your way through it; don't give up on your dream because others do not understand or refuse to support it. Take some time to assess what obstacles are standing in your way real or perceived so can confront them and move forward. Dare to put yourself out there and press your way through until you accomplish your goal. If you truly desire to achieve your goal, figure out a way to go through, over or under, and move whatever obstacles that are in your way so that you can take action now. There is a verse in the Bible that says,

"For verily I say unto you, That whosoever shall say unto this mountain, Be thou removed, and be thou cast into the sea; and shall not doubt in his heart, but shall believe that those things which he saith shall come to pass; he shall have whatsoever he saith." – Mark 11:23 (KJV).

Stand up and face whatever is holding you back—addiction, depression, low self-esteem, fear of failure—or whatever your obstacle. Declare that this is your time, and your opportunity, and you will not be denied. Chip away at your obstacles by finding solutions to deal with them until they are no longer an excuse or reason. Once you move them out the way, if you are serious, you can start the process of working on your goal. *"The truth is, there are only two things in life, reasons, and results, and reasons simply don't count."* – Dr. Mark Anthony. Sometimes if you are unable to get it out your way, you may have to go around it. There was a time when I was faced with a situation that would have taken me several years to obtain my degree if I was not strong-willed, persistent, and determined that I would not be denied or delayed in reaching my goal. I was pursuing my associate degree at New York University, and my director was also pursuing her associate degree at a city college in New York. She was several years my senior. I was attending as a full-time student and she was attending part-time. After learning of my pursuit, she congratulated me and encouraged me. I was even granted a promotion to a supervisory level. All was well until after I graduated with my associate degree and registered for the bachelor's degree program. It was necessary for me to share my higher educational goals with her, because in order for me to receive the partial reimburse benefit from my job, I needed her to sign my tuition reimbursement form prior to registration every semester. During my first semester in the bachelor's program, she commented on the fact that I was going to school full time, and had a full-time position as a supervisor, and that it could be burdensome, and could interfere with my job performance. Never the less, she signed the form, and I was on my way, until the second semester. It was the same scenario, only, this time, she forewarned me that this would be the last time that she was going to be signing a tuition reimbursement form if I continued to attend college as a full-time student. At that point, I felt that my back was against the wall and the goal and timeline I had set for myself was in jeopardy. Sometimes when you are challenged, that's when you become creative. By the third semester, it occurred to me that it wasn't necessary for me to complete the tuition reimbursement form with all my courses; I only needed to submit what I would be reimbursed for. Problem solved—she was happy and I was happy. I continued my full-time studies, in spring, summer, and fall, and graduated with my bachelor's degree within the time I had set for myself to achieve my goal. Her happiness didn't last very long, however, because I completed my bachelor's degree in record time, while she was still attending as a part-time degree student. You may not be able to move every barrier out of your way; you may have to go around them. Sometimes you have to be bullish and not look to the right or to the left until you get to the finish line. Don't place limits on yourself—take the limits off, break down those barriers one by one, and free yourself. When you attempt and succeed at something that you didn't dream was possible, it's like breaking down the bars of your self-imposed prison.

Five Things to
Remind Yourself Daily

I am amazing
I can do anything
Positivity is a choice
I celebrate my individuality
I am prepared to succeed

Fear

Now that you have made some breakthroughs on some of the things that could be holding you back, you should be on your way, right? You might still ask yourself, "But what if I fail?" Don't let fear of failure hold you back. Rebuke the curse of fear. It is said that fear (F.E.A.R.) is *false evidence appearing real.* The sooner you recognize and acknowledge fear for what it is, the sooner you can face it and move forward. Fear is like a growling dog with no teeth. As the saying goes, *all bark and no bite*—that's what fear is. It has no real power over you. The only power that fear has is the power you give it. Fear will take up permanent residency in your mind if you allow it. Serve fear an eviction notice and reclaim your property (your mind). *"Feel the Fear and do it Anyway"* – Susan Jeffers. You must make haste to reach your goal. You cannot get back the time you've lost, so face it, and move on. Fear is one of the main reasons why individuals do not pursue their dreams. So, what if you tried, and it just didn't work out? It just means that you have learned what not to do the next time. Lloyd-Jones said, *"Men who try to do something and fail are infinitely better than those who try to do nothing and succeed."* Work on overcoming your fear of failure. The types of possible fears are numerous. Some of these fears that people encounter when wanting to take action are:

- Fear of failure
- Fear of the unknown
- Fear of being ridiculed
- Fear of success
- Fear of depression
- Fear of lack
- Fear of not being loved
- Fear of abandonment

Kick fear to the curb. Treat fear as you would a liar and a thief; do not harbor it—it will take you down. Fear is a debilitating condition if not conquered will creep into every area of your life. Fear makes you doubt everything, even the very thing you know how to do well. Fear comes in all forms, shapes, and sizes. For instance, fear of public speaking can be crippling and debilitating for some people that as soon as they face their audience and start talking, they shut down. As soon as they realize that all eyes are on them, and the only thing they can hear is the sound of their own voice, they begin to feel faint, even when they have a script or teleprompt. I heard someone say before they overcame their fear of public speaking, they were so terrified if given the choice of being shot or speaking in public, they would have chosen to be shot. It's ok to feel apprehensive, but you shouldn't let it take you out. If you allow fear to take hold, your mind will play tricks on you. It will tell you that you can't achieve your goal. As soon as an obstacle gets in the way, it goes, "Ha, I told you so!" Your mind may tell you that it's too hard, or ask, "What if I fail?" You will be ridiculed or feel stupid. The fear you experience is all in your mind, and your mind wants to keep you protected so you can stay in your comfort zone where it's safe.

So, how do you overcome this disability and the crippling effect that fear has on you? First, you acknowledge that it exists. Second, seek help. Seeking assistance will help you to analyze what is causing the fear so that you can overcome it. The fear may be deep-rooted and stem from years of feeling unsupported or feeling beaten down by life challenges that you've encountered in your past. Negative things may have been said to you by bullies, a parent, teachers or others in authority over you. At some point, you may have subconsciously internalized these negative comments, and, as a result, they lay dormant in the back of your subconscious mind. Just like a dangerous virus, lying in wait for the right time to expose and infect you. Whenever you get close to an opportunity, fear raises its ugly head to remind you of those negative, non-supporting thoughts. As soon as you position yourself and set out to achieve your goal, and you face a barrier, those old memories resurface again. It's been long enough; it's now time to open up that storage area in the back of your mind and empty it out.

Another way to assist you in overcoming fear is to be well prepared. Know your subject matter well. Develop your knowledge to help build your skills and self-confidence. Become an expert—study, do your research, practice, get a mentor. Seek professional assistance to help you overcome your fears. Work on yourself. Tell yourself, "I can do this, and I will do this." Your mind may tell you, "You don't have enough experience. You need to study some more. You need to read another book, take another course, attend another workshop, watch another webinar seminar," and on and on... Don't fall for it. If you have done the work, then do what you know you must do. *Get Started Now!* If you don't, you will stay unfulfilled, year after year, getting older, spending more money, and getting nowhere fast. Well, get over it, and get over yourself. It's not just about you; so, face it, and go for it. Take that leap. You will be better for it. Develop a strong sense of faith and *know that you know that you know.* Recite your affirmation and positive self-talk. Read books and listen to audio recordings that are uplifting and motivational.

Knowing, according to Philippians 4:13: *"I can do all things through Christ which strengthens me."* Don't give up your power to fear. Take charge of your destiny.

> "THERE ISN'T ENOUGH
> ROOM IN YOUR LIFE
> FOR BOTH FEAR AND FAITH.
> EACH DAY, YOU MUST DECIDE
> WHICH ONE GETS TO STAY."
>
> – DAVE WILLIS

Analysis Paralysis

Avoid *analysis paralysis.* Don't over-analyze everything; you become paralyzed by scrutinizing, and accomplish nothing. Over-analyzing is a stalling technique and another form of procrastination due to indecision. *"Procrastination is the bad habit of putting off until the day after tomorrow what should have been done the day before yesterday."* – Napoleon Hill.

You are procrastinating when each topic or idea that you study or explore has no clear result or action taken. Most of the time, the questions that you are asking, you already know the answers to. It's your mind wanting to stall and protect you from entering into unknown territory. Your mind goes through something called "mind freak." It's a protective state of not dealing with the unknown or unchartered territory. The timing or conditions may never be perfect to get started—start anyway. The funding may not come all at once—do something. The more time you spend justifying or stalling, the more time that passes. Days turn into weeks, weeks turn into months, and months turn into years, then on top of if you are getting older and have nothing to show for it. Do your due diligence by developing a checklist and a timeline. Find out all you can, and all that you need to know to get started, and just get started. When you over-analyze, nothing gets done. You are always in a state of preparation and are going to start, but never actually start, therefore, you accomplish nothing.

In order to avoid *analysis paralysis,* you first have to recognize it, acknowledge it, and break out of that behavior. If you are serious about achieving your goal, you must follow-up and follow through on those commitments you made. Take action, no matter how small. Commit to doing at least one thing daily that will assist you in your efforts towards that goal. Every step gets you closer and closer. So go ahead and take a shot at it. So what if you fired and missed your target? Be sure it is in your range, reload, reposition, and fire again; then, repeat.

In this first chapter, we discussed the significance of having a goal and the importance of writing it down. A goal not written is only a wish. Also, you need to develop a process and have a strategic plan in place, then you need to work that plan. We saw that fear and procrastination, if not conquered or controlled, will railroad any well sought-after goal. In Chapter 2, you'll see references and comparisons to individuals with positive and negative outlooks. In addition, we will look at the importance of believing in yourself; because, if you don't believe in yourself, no one else will.

The timing is never perfect. Just start. Then keep going.

Chapter 2

Believe In Yourself

To accomplish your goals, you must believe in yourself. After you have learned the skills and acquired the knowledge necessary to accomplish your goal, go after it with enthusiasm. If things don't seem to be going the way you expect, or everything or everyone appears to be against you, tell yourself, "I can do this," "I will do this," and "I will succeed no matter what." Work to overcome any fear or self-doubt that you may be experiencing. Michael Jordan, who was considered one of the best basketball players of this century said, *"I've missed more than 9000 shots in my career. I've lost almost 300 games. Twenty-six times I've been trusted to take the game-winning shot and missed. I've failed over and over again in my life. And that is why I succeed."* Have a declaration and read it several times a day until you can recite it. Let it resonate in your mind. You must believe whatever you desire before you see it, you must also believe it before you can achieve it. Anything is possible if you believe, so believe.

You must hone in on your skills. Develop yourself by increasing your knowledge and becoming an expert; read, read and read some more. Show yourself as approved; when you do that, you will develop self-confidence in knowing that you are well able, capable, and qualified because you have earned the right.

"Believe in yourself! Have faith in your abilities! Without a humble but reasonable confidence in your own powers, you cannot be successful." – Norman Vincent Peale

If you don't believe in yourself, you cannot expect others to believe in you. When you believe in yourself, your whole attitude changes and it doesn't matter what others may say or feel about you. Your posture—the way you carry yourself—changes. You're so full of self-confidence that you can be spotted from across the room. Venus Williams said: *"Some people say I have attitude—maybe I do...but I think you have to. You have to believe in yourself when no one else does—that makes you a winner right there."*

GET a Mentor or an Accountability Partner

To assist you on your journey to reach your goal, you need support along the way. To be successful and avoid some of the pitfalls that could come as a result of trial and error, get a support team in your corner that you can rely on to help guide you. You need a mentor, a coach, and an accountability partner. You should have at least one, or all three if possible, depending on your need. These individuals can give you guidance and support, and empower you regarding your:

· Self-confidence
· Finances
· Relationships
· Goals

Your mentor could be your former high school teacher, coach, or boss. Ask yourself, who you know, or who someone else knows, that possesses the experience and knowledge that would be a good mentor to you. They could help you to do a personal S.W.O.T. (Strength Weakness Opportunities and Threats) of your personal life to identify your needs and where you need help the most. SWOT analysis is a tool used in business to identify and access the strength or vulnerabilities of the business. A coach could assist you in the planning of your goals, after identifying your strengths, to capitalize on them and work through your weaknesses, turning them into advantages. How have they served you and others around you? Where has it gotten you at this point in your life and how will it help you to achieve your goals? Recognize and face your weakness so that you can deal with it and get past it. How has it held you back, and how much power does it have over you? Do you see the opportunities when they present themselves to you or do you recognize them after they have slipped past you? Threats are those things or people that get in the way of your success; how you plan to deal with them, fix them, or get rid of them, is very important.

A mentor can also help you to identify things that may be mentally blocking you and holding you back from taking action. You may feel like a mouse on a wheel, going around and around, not knowing what to do or how to get off. Your mentor could help you shift your focus and guide you to a smoother path. Be open to suggestions from your mentor and accountability partners. You don't know what you don't know. When you allow outside intervention and you share your goals, it will help you get unstuck and enable you to look at things from a different angle or from a different perspective. Even if you don't take their advice, it will broaden your thinking and allow you to expand your thoughts in areas you probably otherwise wouldn't if you did not have a sounding board, so stay open-minded.

Your support team should be made up of people you trust and who want what's best for you, they want you to grow and succeed. They need to have different roles and skill sets. They can help you to keep your commitment to yourself and to stick to your goal as you chip away at each phase of the blueprint.

You need individuals who are not going to judge you—people who will give you constructive criticism and steer you in the right direction. Get someone who will be honest with you and not afraid to tell you the truth. They will *call you out* when you are not doing what you said you were going to do when you were going to do it. That person will remind you what it is costing you if you fail to follow through. If you get off course, they will be there to get you back on track.

Form Healthy Relationships

Having healthy relationships is important when working on your goal. There is a saying: *"No man is an island."* Everyone needs someone in their corner. Surround yourself with individuals from various backgrounds. Just as the saying goes, *"It takes a village to raise a child,"* for you, it may take an army to help you to reach your goal. Develop and maintain good relationships with people that you know will support you. Have people on your team who have supported you in the past, and you know, based on their actions, they will give you encouragement, and you can rely on them. They will give you feedback or constructive criticism, and point out your blind spots. They will be there to encourage and motivate you to pursue your goals. You have others that you know who truly love you and have your best interest at heart. You need to have people in your corner who, if you slack off or get off track, will show you some tough love, and to whom you are answerable. Get individuals who you know will assist you in getting through the finish line, and, even if you fall down and skin your knees, they won't let you stay down they are going to tell you to get up, brush yourself off, and keep going; cry about it later, but, right now, you need to keep going until you get through to the finish line. I once had a tennis partner, every time we played together we always won. One day I tripped and fell on the court while running to hit a short drop shot. She was so competitive and focus on winning, all I heard was her loud commanding voice shouting, "GET UP." I did however recover and hit the next shot to win the point. It's not because she didn't care that I may have been hurt, her focus was, we are a winning team, we have skills to win the match, so we don't have time for self-pity, get up hit the next shot and win the point, we'll tend to any injury after.

Associate yourself not only with champions in your corner but also with individuals who are trustworthy and have moral integrity. Don't take shortcuts or engage in any type of behavior that could be skewed as being dubious. Be selective and intentional with whom you choose to build your relationships with. Choose individuals who, that as a result of their qualities, success, and talents, can help to catapult you to the next level. Be sure that they share your dreams, and, if they do, these individuals will bring different and fresh new ideas that you may not have thought of. In addition, as a result of your engaging with them, you will learn, as well as grow, in the process. You may be saying to yourself, "Yes, that sounds great. I wish I had people like that in my immediate circle. I don't know individuals like that. How would I meet them? Where would I start?" I'm so glad you asked. In this day of social media and network marketing, it's not that difficult; however, you need to be intentional about it. It's not just going to happen through "osmosis." You have to be deliberate, intentional; and you have to take action.

By the same token, it's okay to admire someone who has achieved success and the qualities that you aspire to have but do not compare yourself to other people, especially those on social media sites. You may feel that you don't measure up, but what they are portraying may be a facade.

"SURROUND YOURSELF ONLY WITH PEOPLE WHO ARE GOING TO TAKE YOU HIGHER"

– Oprah Winfrey

Stay Away from Negative People

Surround yourself with positive people who love and support you, and believe in your dream. To realize your dream, you may have to distance yourself from those family members and friends who are not supportive. You may even have to change your environment. Stay away from negative people. It's not that they are mean-spirited; it is just their way of coping with the world and their surroundings. Those types of people always see the glass as half full, and if you hang around them long enough, you will too. Most negative people have been that way most of their lives, but we don't usually pay close attention to them. Once you have developed a sense of awareness, and decide to move in a different direction in order to change your circumstances and commit to self-improvement, their negative outlook on life becomes more evident. You begin to realize that this outlook is bad for you and that this type of behavior is toxic and does not support your way of thinking. Then, there are the bearers of bad news. Those are people who are always the first to hear when something bad happens, and they can't wait to share it with everyone that they meet. There are also those who, no matter what day of the week, month, or year in which you talk to them, there is some type of drama going on in their lives. So much so, that when they are through unloading their life baggage on you, you become depressed. Sometimes these negative people are the people closest to you, such as family members, or even a parent. It is even worse if they live with you. It may be that you have no choice but to hear their doom and gloom stories repeatedly because they have been telling the same stories for years. If you're unable to physically get away from them, you may have to find a way to escape them mentally. Once you become aware of the situation, you are able to take action and do something about it, and, by taking action, that action could lead to the type of change which you are seeking.

You don't have to watch or listen to every news report either. Some of us catch the 6 a.m., 5 p.m., 6 p.m., and 11 p.m. news, and also read about it via the Internet. We are so bombarded with negative news that it stunts our creativity and positive outlook. It is hard to stay positive and uplifted when we are constantly listening to the negative news, sometimes first thing before we start our day, and last thing before we go to bed at night. By the way, just in case we missed anything, there are the "news mongers" that can't wait to tell you again about the *good/bad* news that we missed. Please know that these bearers of bad news are sensationalists who are paid handsomely. They also receive awards for depressing you. The more you watch or listen to it, the more their high ratings are boosted—all that means to them is *cha-ching, cha-ching.*

Mayo Clinic Study

The mayo clinic conducted a study asking individuals whether they saw a glass as half empty or half full. The objective was to see how this common phrase, that's been used by many for so long, signifies if someone is optimistic or pessimistic. They are of the belief that how someone chooses to answer that question not only indicates their outlook on life or themselves but could have a negative impact on their health.

Other studies also indicate that your personality trait of either being positive or and negative can affect many areas of your health and happiness. The positive thinking that typically comes with optimism is a key part of effectively controlling stress. Being able to control stress levels has direct health benefits. If you are generally negative, you need not worry; you can learn and develop positive thinking skills.

Thinking positive usually, begins with self-talk. These self-talks are constant and continuous thoughts flowing in your mind. These streams of thoughts can be positive or negative. It' a wildly held belief that you develop your self-talk through logic and reason. On the other hand, other self-talk could be a result of misconceptions that you produce due to lack of information. It was indicated that if the thoughts that run through your head are mostly negative, it is believed that your way of viewing the world is negative. However, if your thoughts are generally positive, you're likely an optimist and often engage in positive thinking.

According to the Mayo Clinic study, some of the health benefits of positive thinking are:

- Longer life span
- Lower rate of depression
- Lower levels of distress
- Greater resistance to the common cold
- Better psychological and physical well-being
- Reduced risk of death from cardiovascular disease
- Better coping skills during hardships and times of stress

Now that you have insight into how being optimistic vs pessimistic can impact your health and happiness, it would be helpful to be able to identify or recognize when you or someone you care about may be engaging in that type of unhealthy behavior.

Here are some examples to help you identify whether your self-talk is positive or negative:

- **Filtering.** You amplify the bad aspects of a circumstance and ignore the positive. For example, if you were complimented on a job well done, as well as having completed it ahead of schedule, instead of savoring the moment by acknowledging the compliment, you are dismissive and instead, immediately focus on doing even more.

- **Personalizing.** You blame yourself for everything that goes wrong. As an example, your night out with friends was canceled, so you immediately assume that it has something to do with you.

- **Catastrophizing.** Your outlook on everything is usually pessimistic. If something doesn't go your way at the start of your day, you automatically assume that it sets the tone for the rest of your day.

- **Polarizing.** You see things as black or white; there are no gray areas. If things don't go your way, you are a total disaster.

Concentrate on the Positive

It is possible to turn your negative thinking around to a positive one. The study said that it can be learned, but it will take time, just as forming any new habit takes time. Below are some ways to turn your negative thinking into ways of being more positive:

- **Think about areas you would like to change.**
  Start by changing the way in which you view things, and practice thinking more positive. Take baby steps.

Start by identifying one thing; it could be the way you feel about your job, family, lack of money, or something simple, as long as you realize that you are shifting your thinking from viewing it negatively to positively.

· **Check yourself.**
Throughout your day, take the opportunity and consciously think positive, and, should you find yourself having a negative thought, replace it with a positive one.

· **Be open to humor.**
It may be difficult at times, but laughing relieves stress. So, when you feel overwhelmed, try laughing. Laugh at yourself, or the situation you find yourself in. Develop a good sense of humor.

· **Follow a healthy lifestyle.**
Develop an exercise routine. Exercise about three times a week. It is not only good for your health; it reduces stress and it rejuvenates you, both in mind and body, and makes you feel happy.

· **Surround yourself with positive people.**
Be selective, and associate with people who you know will love and support you and your efforts. Negative people will drain you, and rob you of your peace and your joy, and contribute nothing to your growth.

Negative people will stress you out.

•

- **Practice positive self-talk.** Begin every day with a daily affirmation or a positive quote. Say things like, "Today is going to be a great day!" If something negative comes to mind, immediately replace it with a positive thought. Don't be too hard on yourself; it's a process. Put things in perspective; evaluate why you viewed it that way and put a positive spin on it. Be kind to yourself.

If you are generally negative, below are some examples from the Mayo Clinic Staff to encourage you to practice positive self-talk:

Negative Self-Talk	Positive Thinking
• I've never done it before.	• It's an opportunity to learn something new.
• It's too complicated.	• I'll tackle it from a different angle.
• I don't have the resources.	• Necessity is the mother of invention.
• I'm too lazy to get this done.	• I wasn't able to fit it into my schedule, but I can re-examine some priorities.
• There is no way it will work.	• I can try to make it work.
• It's too radical.	• Let's take a chance.
• No one bothers to communicate with me.	• I'll see if I can open the channel of communication.
• I'm not going to get any better at this.	• I'll give it another try.

Practice Daily to Think Positive

It's a work in progress, so do not expect that you will suddenly become positive overnight. However, with practice, you will gradually make progress. Practice positive self-talk daily. Do not be critical of yourself or view the world around you negatively all the time.

When you reprogram your mind to think and react positively, you are better able to handle stressful situations more rationally, and that contributes to a healthier you.

DRAMA

DOES NOT JUST WALK
INTO YOUR LIFE.
YOU EITHER CREATE IT,
INVITE IT,
OR YOU ASSOCIATE WITH PEOPLE
WHO LOVE TO BRING IT
INTO YOUR LIFE.

– Unknown

Start Where You Are

Many individuals have a dream inside them, something they would like to give birth to, but they are afraid to even try. They have no idea where to start, so they continue to let it float around in limbo or just continue to talk about it. If you feel that you truly have something that you feel passionate about, and it's a burning desire, get moving. We are in the technological age where access to information is limitless. Take advantage of all the various opportunities that are available through books, social media, and groups. Start where you are; through study and consistent learning, you'll become very knowledgeable. There are countless ways to do research, and numerous opportunities available to gain information, that has minimal to no cost to get started. You owe it to yourself, as well as to others who could benefit from pursuing it. Everything is not going to be perfect. It's OK to just start where you are. Follow the steps to actualize it. Free yourself from your self-imposed barriers, and don't let your dream die with you. In Jeremiah 29:11, it says: *for I know the plans I have for you," declares the LORD, "plans to prosper you and not to harm you, plans to give you hope and a future.* New International Version

In this chapter, we looked at believing in yourself and the importance of tapping into your resources by asking for help. We also looked at staying away from negative people and influences that could contaminate or sabotage your thinking. The study conducted by the mayo clinic illustrated how a negative vs positive outlook can significantly change the quality of your life. Another important factor is to stop waiting for the perfect conditions to start working on your goals, start where you are. The next chapter will be addressing the significance of thinking and remaining positive throughout the process.

The most effective way to do it, is to do it.

- Amelia Earhart

Chapter 3

Think Positive

Think positive thoughts. Imagine that you have accomplished your goal, and go about acting as if it were already done, knowing that if you believe it, you can achieve it, and what you focus on, expands. Don't let anyone deter you or let you feel unworthy or unqualified. Plant that seed in your mind and water it daily with positive affirmations. Find some quiet time and be still—so still that the only thing you hear is the rhythmic beat of your heart. During those quiet moments, purge your mind of the hustle and bustle of the day, so that when you rise, you will feel refreshed and feel renewed. Practice meditating and praying. Pray in silence. Praying doesn't have to be out loud. In your solitary moments, you gain inner strength and have a better outlook on your situations. During your one on one with God, pray earnestly for what you want. Profess that you have already received it, and then give him thanks as if it were already granted. Then, when you rise from your moment of solitude, go to work, and do your part to make it happen, and receive what you prayed for. Because faith equals works *"...faith without works, is dead." –* James 14:26 (KJV).

The more positive you are, the less likely that you will take on stress. When you are stressed, minor incidents can *take you out.* Those minor incidents can build up and begin to cause health issues. An accumulation of those health issues, over time, could even result in disease such as cancer. That is why it is vitally important to find positive ways in which to ward off trivial, everyday incidents, and develop a way to put a positive spin on it. Doing so could very well save your life.

At the start of each day, make a commitment to think positive thoughts. This may be a tough challenge when everyone around you seems to be doing the opposite— the news reports from everything overnight, the traffic report, weather, politics or whatever. Before you engage in all the negative stimuli around, take a moment to give thanks for the life that you have and at least one thing that you are thankful for. Send a positive message to your brain to combat all the negative things that you may encounter throughout the day. Get recharged. Spend a few minutes reprogramming your mind to think positive thoughts. Replace old negative thoughts with positive ones. Visualize yourself having a productive and successful day. When you do, you are sending signals to your brain to say that this is what you want and that nothing else will suffice. Start seeing the glass as half full. You will somehow look for the positive spin, or the good, that can come from every situation as a result. It is said that thoughts are things, so think positive in order to change your mindset.

Frederique Murphy said, *"When you master your mindset, you free yourself to achieve the level of success you desire."* It may appear as if all hell is breaking loose around you; just know that it's part of the tuition you pay to get you to where you are heading. If you choose to blow up every time you face a difficult or unfair situation, you're going to have a miserable life. So, if you want to live a life that is less stressful, control the way that you choose to deal with challenges and stress. Take a few seconds to breathe and to think about the best way to deal with the negative situations. You control your thoughts; therefore, you alone can determine your reaction to any situation, on any given day. If you are one to be explosive when you face challenges, do yourself a personal favor and calm down; nothing is worth sacrificing your health, and, ultimately, your life for. Do a challenging exercise, for at least seven days, where you replace your negative thought with a positive, and use phrases, such as, "This too shall pass." Before you react, say something positive; master your thinking and your words. Words have *life*. They have power, and they become your reality, so, *speak life*. Say what you want and how you want it to be. Speak the words. There are so many examples in the Bible that refer to the power of the spoken words! One verse says, *"Death and life are in the power of the tongue, and they that love it shall eat the fruit thereof."* – Proverbs 18:21 (KJV). You can choose to speak words of encouragement, or you can choose words of defeat—the choice is yours.

Speaking words of encouragement is like watering a seed that has been planted. If you desire to successfully reach your goal, you should always speak positively about it, and prophecy about it, until it becomes a reality. Speak only words of encouragement over your life. You should not only say it, you must also believe it. You must already see yourself having whatever you desire and believe that you deserve it. Because words have such power, daily affirmations are extremely important. On a daily basis, you should say out loud, "This is a good day. Something good is going to happen to me today. This is the day that the Lord has made. I will rejoice and be glad in it." You should have a word, a verse, or a quote; have something that, when things are not going the way you would like them to, you can say, and it will uplift, strengthen, and encourage you. Listening to inspiring and positive messages can calm and comfort you in times of uncertainty. When I was a little girl, and things would not be working in our favor, my mother would say to me, "It will be long, but not forever." When I got older, and I would get into situations where I could not see my way out, or how and when it would end, I would hear her voice, and those comforting words would come back to me as an anchor and a support—"it will be long, but not forever." Those words brought me such comfort and peace because I would stop looking at the current circumstances, and, instead, focus on the resolution.

Yes, You Can

Yes, you can, but you've got to BELIEVE before you can achieve. Successful people are passionate about their goals. They are persistent, they are resilient, and they are adaptable in their thinking. They are focused. They know the desired outcome they are seeking, and it won't happen by chance, but by deliberate intention. If what they desire isn't going the way they initially perceived it would go; they take another route, but they don't give up. For them, there is no such thing as, "Well, I tried that and it didn't work, so I gave up." No, they keep trying until they find what works. Sometimes it may be the very thing that they have tried before, but maybe the timing wasn't right, and maybe they needed to approach it from a different angle. They keep doing and doing until they make progress. Even though you know you can, don't think for a second that your mind won't play tricks on you. That part of your mind that wants to keep you safe will whisper, "Do you really think you can do it? What if you fail? What if your friends or critics laugh at you? Maybe you are not cut out for that."

Like Les Brown said, *"Sometimes you have to tell your mind, SHUT UP,"* in order to stop the noise in your head so that you can think and have clarity. You have to empty your mind and get rid of the clutter attempting to sabotage your success. You have to replace it with thoughts of positive self-talk and visualization of what you are desiring to achieve. It's important to talk to yourself, but be sure that you are telling yourself the right stuff. What you tell yourself, or focus on, is what you will attract; therefore, speaking to yourself is also manifesting over your life or your situation. When you get out of bed, acknowledge by paying homage to a higher power, or whatever, or whoever, you believe is keeping you. After you've shown your gratitude, then tell yourself, "No matter what, today I'm going to have a great day." When you do that, your brain says, "OK!" Start looking for the positives, even in the most negative of circumstances. Just by planting that seed, you generate a positive flow of energy, power, and focus. No, it's not all going to be smooth sailing all the way. You may encounter turbulence; you may run into some "Grinch." Do not indulge them; keep them at bay, just give them a quick hello—and a quicker goodbye—and keep on going.

You can train your brain to think of the things and areas you desire, in order to succeed at the things you desire. You know you can do it, so what is the problem? You may ask yourself, "Why do I feel stuck? I have all the tools and the resources, and I am capable, so, why am I not further along? That is because you may have to change the way in which you view things, and the questions that you are asking yourself, as well as the information you may subconsciously allow to seep into your brain. Whether or not you are aware of it, it is said that the brain processes 70,000 + thoughts a day, depending on whose scientific study you read. You have the ability to channel some of those thoughts and use them to help you achieve your goal. So, it may not be enough just to plant the seed of *"yes I can."* You also have to water it and fertilize it so that it can have the nourishment to grow and develop in order to get the outcome that you desire. One way to do that is to do brain exercises.

- On a daily basis, practice positive thinking. If a negative thought pops into your mind, immediately replace it with a positive thought.

- Change your focus. *"Whatever the mind can conceive and believe, it can achieve."* – Napoleon Hill. You would be amazed how, once you decide to change your focus and pay attention to a particular item or topic, all of a sudden, it seems to be all around you. That's why you need to focus on what you want, not on what you don't want, so that you can draw to yourself whatever you desire.

- Think of some of the things and/or people in your life for whom you are grateful, and why.

- Don't be a worrier; it's futile and doesn't serve any purpose.

- Be a giver. Sow into the lives of other people, and share with others as much as you are able to.

You can't control other people, but you can change your attitude of how you choose to deal with them.

You may be the product of a negative environment where everyone seems to have the same non-supporting way of thinking. The fact that you recognized that this type of behavior, and way of thinking, has not served you, and you desire to change, you are a winner. Winners never quit. Now you need to get up, get out, take action, and get it done. Your proactive mind might say:

- But what if I fail?

- If I succeed, could I handle it?

- I may lose some friends; I won't have time to socialize.

- My family may not support my ideas.

All that may be true—keep going anyway.

I can recall several examples of how powerful the mind can be when you focus and direct your attention to something that you really want. On my first vacation visit from New York to Atlanta, I immediately fell in love with the southern hospitality. I was so excited about the place that when I went back to New York, that was all I thought about. I imagined buying one of the new homes that were being built all over the metro Atlanta area. However, reality kicked in; I had no money—not even for a down payment. It seemed so out of reach, and such a stretch, due to a lack of finances, being a newly-divorced, single mom of two small children, and on and on. Nevertheless, the dream would not die; it got even stronger. I went back during another vacation and viewed more houses, toured the city, and visited several attractions; however, my circumstances hadn't changed much from the previous year. I started imagining the type of house that I wanted, and I imagined myself going from room to room. I imagined seeing myself and my children playing in the backyard. On our second visit, one of the things that my friends and I did was to stop at a garage sale. I purchased a novelty sprinkler head for kids, the type that when hooked to a hose, the kids would have fun wetting themselves on hot summer days while playing in the backyard. I did not take it back home to New York but left it at my friend's home because it would not have been of any use in an apartment in Brooklyn, New York.

My friends videotaped all our tours of the new homes' and open house events. They gave me a copy of the videotape to take back to New York. Our desire to move to Atlanta was so very strong that on Sunday afternoons during family relaxation time, we would all gather around the television and watch the video of the Atlanta home tour, over and over again, and, every time we saw it, we acted as though it were for the first time. That was our only entertainment for months.

Maintaining my enthusiasm, I was on my way to work one morning when a section of a song by Bob Marley popped into my head: "Baby, don't worry about a thing, cause every little thing is going to be all right." I got so excited; the next thing that came to mind was, *call your friends and ask them to find a realtor.* I felt as though I had won the lottery. Nine months later, I gave birth to it; I had my home in Atlanta, and it was more than I thought I would have. Whatever you focus on, expands. As Esther Jno-Charles says, *"Focus on what you want, not on what you don't want."* If you desire, and you are truly determined to reach your goal, you will become unstoppable. Go to work and do all that you can to make it happen. You will find a way, where at first there seemed to be no way. You will find those things you thought were obstacles are suddenly moving out of your way. According to Les Brown, *"You have to be HUNGRY."* To reach your goal, you must first visualize yourself having it. When you open yourself up that way, everything else falls into place; all your energy moves forward and goes to work to make it happen.

Watch What You Say

Another reason to think positive and say positive things about yourself is when you do you are causing it to come to pass. It may seem like harmless words, but be very careful of what you say. There is a saying: *"Be careful what you wish for; you may get it."*

I recalled as a 12 years old in Jamaica walking home from school with a group of friends one evening. We were fantasying about our future. Like we always did, we played around and imagined a lot of things. I particularly recalled this one evening, talking about what we were going to be when we grew up. Everyone was dreaming of being some type of professional, owning big homes, driving big cars, and so on. I knew I wanted all that and more, so very convincingly, I blurted out, *"I'm going to America,"* as if it was a done deal and everything had already been arranged. Everyone turned to look at me as if to say, "Sure you are," and then continued talking. Of course, I was unaware of any family member that was already there or had the resources needed to get me there. It was only a dream. To me, going to America meant that all my dreams could come true-but it seemed an impossible dream. It appeared out of reach and too audacious. From what I knew, people who went to America all came back rich. When they came back to visit they were able to afford anything they wanted. They had the biggest houses, drove the best cars, and wore the best clothes. But for me, and my family, it seemed out of reach—or so I thought.

Fast forwarding about two years later, my mom came to me and asked, "How would you like to go to America?" I was stunned. My mother had a sense of humor, but a practical joker she was not. I paused for a moment to comprehend what I had just heard, and replied, "Yes," still in a daze. She went on to explain that my dad was living in the United States he came home to visit. He approached her and asked if she would allow me to come live with him in the United States. I didn't grow up with him or had any knowledge of his whereabouts. About a year and a half later, I was there and the rest is history.

"And I say unto you, Ask, and it shall be given you; seek, and ye shall find; knock, and it shall be opened unto you." – St Luke 11:9.

When you speak words of faith, and of hope and encouragement, there are forces, angels waiting to grant it. Your angel is standing by listening to what you are saying or asking, so it can start working on your behalf. So, think positive, and dream big. It doesn't cost you anything to dream, but it could cost you if you don't. So, dream on. By the same token, speak negatively and you could experience things that you don't want to invite into your life; so, dismiss negative thoughts when they creep into your mind. Plush them out, do not entertain them and don't you dare verbalize them.

Take Small Bites

How do you eat an elephant? One bite at a time. Take small bites; arrange big goals into smaller ones. Map out a step-by-step process of how you plan to achieve your goal, and design a blueprint of the process necessary to achieve it. In that way, it will not seem so overwhelming. In other words, your elephant will be more palatable as well as manageable. When you are clear about your objectives, you can imagine the possibilities. If you have laid a solid foundation by creating a blueprint and a realistic timeline, it will be much easier to accomplish. Don't think about the journey as for where you are or how much farther you have to go; do as much as you can to complete each step in the process. Each step no matter how small gets you one step closer.

As a competitive tennis player, I love winning. Sometimes I find myself down in a game or in a set. I found that when I stop focusing on my score and begin to focus on the current point being played, many times I have come back from behind to win; even though I thought the person I was playing had a better game than I did. During those instances, all I do is to tell myself repeatedly, *"One point at a time."* No matter how things are looking at the moment, one point at a time leads to victory, and *Game, Set, Match.* Formulate your goals into small bites. Design a written game plan. Arrange each section of your goal into smaller manageable goals. Be sure that they are achievable and realistic. Work on each part within the timeline that you set for yourself. Each time you accomplish a portion, check it off; when you do, you will feel like a champion. It will build momentum and enthusiasm, and as you progress to the next level, you will be so much happier and have more self-confidence.

So, in Chapter 3, you saw how having a positive mindset could propel you to a higher level of thinking, and it also made you aware that anything is possible if you believe. As important as having a positive mindset are the words you use, and what you say constantly and consistently. Therefore, take hold of your thoughts as well as your words, and speak positively about every area of your life. In addition, taking small deliberate steps will help you to manage your time and tasks more successfully, without feeling overwhelmed. Moving into Chapter 4, you will see, if you are serious and intentional about your goal, you will do what's necessary to obtain it.

Chapter 4

Get Serious

Get serious. What are some of the things that are really important to you? What do you want to improve on? What do you need help with most? Is what you want in line with the overall theme of your goals? If it is something that requires the help and assistance of others, what is the first step of approach in reaching him or her in order to get their assistance? Is there a gatekeeper? How do you plan to get their attention? Get advice from those who have already done it. If you are truly serious about reaching your goal, you have to get serious. Cut to the chase, cut out the excuses because there will be many. There will always be good reasons why you can't get things done as you anticipate you would. Make up your mind that you will do whatever it takes to reach your goal. You have to develop a dogged attitude when it comes to the *stick-to-itiveness*—you will see it through no matter what. Invest in yourself. One of the best investments you can make is in yourself. It's a belief that at least 3–5% of your annual income should be allocated for your self-development. Learn all that you can; build a library of books, videos, audio readers and other sources regarding your topics of interest.

Earl Nightingale said, *"If you study one hour a day in your field of interest, in three years you will master it. If you commit to studying like that, in five years you will become an expert, and, in seven years, one of the best in the world in your field."* Take courses, and attend seminars and conferences. Hang around like-minded individuals. There is a saying; birds of a feather flock together, and Jim Rohn said, *"You are the average of the five people you spend the most time with."* Seek out, and join, networking, meet-ups, masterminds and inner-circle groups. These individuals have the same mindset as you, and they will keep you motivated and inspired. Do whatever it takes to get you closer to your goal. It may not happen overnight, but if you are intentional about the steps required to get you there, then don't delay; do it now.

Mind your own business. Don't pay attention to what others are doing. Work on yourself. Do something daily that will get you closer to your goal. Check in with yourself daily by asking if what you are doing right now is contributing to your mission of achieving your goal. Don't waste time worrying about things you can't control; let it go, and resolve the things that you can do something about. Refer back to your blueprint daily, and chart your progress. Are you on target, or do you need to pick up the pace?

There are certain habits you should incorporate daily to keep you on task. *"95% of everything we do is a result of habit."* – Aristotle. Practice daily goal setting. List each task, in order of priority, the night before. What are those activates that must get done if nothing else. Keep a daily journal. Journaling also helps to keep you focused and motivated. The reason why most people never reach their goals is that they don't define them, learn about them, or even seriously consider them as believable or achievable. *"Winners can tell you where they are going, what they plan to do along the way, and who will be sharing the adventure with them."* – Denis Waitley

You Must Be Self-Disciplined

To achieve your goals, you must be self-disciplined. The dictionary version of self-discipline is: *"the ability to control one's own feelings and overcome one's weaknesses."*

Self-discipline plays a major role in achieving your goal. You will get out what you put in. Lack of self-discipline can railroad your goals; you can easily go off track and revert back to your natural habits because it's easier to do. Whatever you are used to doing on a daily basis comes naturally and without thinking. We are creatures of habit; therefore, we subconsciously do certain things without thinking. As an example, I drive to work the same way every day. I put no thought or effort into where I need to go or turn; I just do it automatically. Every turn I need to make is so deeply ingrained into my subconscious, I know all the potholes or bumps in the road. I am so sensitive to the holes that I automatically, without any thought, drive around them to avoid hitting them. So deep are they in my subconscious that, even after the potholes were fixed, I found myself still driving around the spot to avoid hitting them. Because I had been doing it for some time, it took a conscious effort to remember that it was OK to drive straight, and not go around where the holes once was. In much the same way, to develop self-discipline, it takes a conscious and deliberate effort to do those things you are not accustomed to.

You must discipline yourself to consciously do those things that are not routine until they become habits.

Self-discipline is a key component and usually requires sacrifice. Some things you are used to doing may have to be put on hold, or be given up altogether when working on your goal. You may not be able to be the life of the party or the social butterfly that you are used to being. You may not be able to entertain or go to the movies as much. You may even have to skip a few important events such as family reunion if it conflicts with your timeline. The price you pay on the front-end will pay off on the back-end. If you are truly serious about achieving your goal, you have to develop tunnel vision; no one will need to push you. The fact is, you may have to be slowed down after you get revved up. However, if you develop a blueprint and stick to the timeline as much as possible, you will successfully finish your journey. Also, if you find yourself drifting aimlessly, deviating, or wandering off, keep a calendar. Log the top ten things you must do, then from that, choose the most important two and do them first.

Be willing to work hard for what you want. Be a shameless promoter for your goals. Be willing to put in the time and effort to see it through. Sacrifices will have to be made; it is all part of the cost. Despite setbacks, roadblocks or pushbacks—those challenges that show up in your life to slow you down—just know it is part of the life lessons. When it's all said and done, it will serve to strengthen and add to your life experience. Anything worth having is worth fighting for. If it was so easy, everyone would do it, but they won't. Why? Because most people will not push themselves beyond their limit. If you want it badly enough, then don't ever give up; don't quit fighting for what you want. When you put yourself on the line, failure is not an option. Note that the only person that can really stop you, is you, so don't put limits on yourself or your abilities.

Get in the right mindset. Speak what you want, into *existence*. Reprogram your mind to think positive and act as if it were already achieved. Get your words and your thoughts, and your visualization, all in sync. You are the best defense you have against anything that can come against you. Should you encounter any non-supporting thoughts or setbacks, and that little voice starts to tell you that it's too hard, just use your imagination—we all have one for a reason. When you start to imagine the possibilities, your subconscious will say, "Yes, I can see it now." Then, your conscious mind will join in telling it, "Let's go do it."

Keep Your Eye on the Prize

"The credit belongs to the man who is actually in the arena; whose face is marred by dust and sweat and blood; who strives valiantly; who errs and comes short again and again; who knows the great enthusiasms, the great devotions, and spends himself in a worthy cause; who at the best knows in the end the triumph of high achievement; and who at the worst, if he fails, at least fails while daring greatly." – Theodore Roosevelt

Keep your eye on the prize. Don't lose focus; when you stay focused on your goal, you will make more progress than when you deviate from it. Life happens. No matter how much you plan or prepare, things are going to happen that may be beyond your control— it's called life. How you choose to react to it will make all the difference. It could make or break you. Therefore, when you are presented with a life-challenging situation, deal with it the best way you know how, but keep moving. Decide not to exert unnecessary energy over situations for which you have no control. It will exhaust you and wear you down. Instead, put things in perspective; evaluate its severity and deal with it accordingly. If it is a challenging situation that must be dealt with immediately, or cannot be postponed, take care of it, and then get back on track.

Sometimes we allow minor tasks to interfere with our timeline for accomplishing our big goal. There are times when those little "to-do's" gnaw at you, and keep on popping up in your mind until you do them. It could be that some of those minor tasks need attending to so that they don't escalate into something bigger later; however, some minor tasks can be put on the back burner. For instance, you hadn't had a chance to check your emails all day, so you decide to scan through to ensure significant alerts or notifications are not missed. But, instead of viewing those and going back to the others later, as you told yourself, you keep on opening, reading, and responding, and clicking on their attached links or directions to their Facebook page, or other websites. Before you realize it, hours of your valuable time have passed, and you have nothing to show for it. Many times we avoid doing things that we should because it is not fun. Your brain likes doing fun stuff; it loves pleasure. When your brain goes into pleasure mode, it doesn't recognize the time, and it knows no boundaries. What you have to do to achieve your goal may not be fun or pleasurable, but it is crucial to your future and to your success.

Prioritize your life. Put first things first. Put in the *big rocks* first. In Stephen Covey's book, *"7 Habits of Highly Successful People,"* he spoke about taking care of the most essential things in your life first. At one of his seminars, he had an attendee assist him to illustrate his emphasis of prioritizing life's most essential things first. If you don't do that, you will run out of time and make it more difficult to reach your goals successfully. On the table, he had a large jar, some sand, gravel, and some big rocks. He asked the attendee to put the items in the large jar.

First, was the placement of the sand: That was done quickly and effortlessly.

Second, the gravel: This was done in quite the same manner, with no challenges.

Third, the big rocks: The first two or so went in okay; however, the other big and most important rocks, representing life's essentials (family, relationships, career), could not be put in successfully because there was not enough room left in the jar to fit them. The sand and gravel (less essential task) that was placed in the jar first, took the space that would allow the big rocks, (the most important and essential things in your life), to fit in the jar successfully and effortlessly.

To make his point, he had the attendee remove the contents from the jar, and asked if anything could be done differently. The demonstration was repeated again, and, this time, the big rocks were placed in the jar first, then the gravel, and, next, the sand. To everyone's amazement, all the contents fit easily and effortlessly. It goes to show, when we neglect to prioritize our (Big Rocks) most essential things in our lives, we miss opportunities, it makes our life more difficult, which results in stress and anxiety. Choose to set your priorities and work towards getting them done first. Don't sweat the small stuff; you will be happier and much more productive.

First things first: Take care of those most important things in your life; if not, you will find that you may run out of time, and or money. Do what needs to be done.

http//:www.bigrockideas.com

Look at the big picture. Practice good time management. Take the time to do the most important things in your life first. What are those priorities or important areas of your life—spiritual, family, career—that, if not taken care of in a timely and consistent manner, could sabotage all your effort? After the most important things are taken care of, focus on the smaller, non-essential things in your life. Many people tend to pay too much attention to the minor things that do not yield many results, and neglect essential things, rendering them out of focus and therefore missing their target. Take control of your time. Avoid procrastination and take actions that will push you further towards accomplishing your goal. Remind yourself why you want your goal, and think of how it will make you feel once you have achieved it.

Quotesvalley.com

Go All In

If you desire to experience massive success and achieve your goal, go all in. Commit yourself to doing just that and watch what happens. Throw your whole self into it, holding nothing back. When you become so laser focus, you will be amazed how your mind starts opening up and ideas start to flow. You will think of creative ways of accomplishing your goals. When you do, it will seem like out of nowhere things just start happening in your favor. You will begin to get new ideas. You can't contain yourself—you become energized, your adrenalin starts to flow, and you generate new strength. Remember, the mind believes anything you tell it. Therefore, when you go to work to achieve it, your mind goes to work and follow suit. Then, your mind will be asking you, "What took you so long? I knew you could do it." You will want to push yourself further and faster. It's like God saying, "OK, you have done your part, now let me. Move over so that I can add my *super* to your *natural*, to give you supernatural abilities that you can use to move forward. Then He begins to make a way where at first you didn't see a way. Then, all you have to do is stay on the path and continue the journey. Throughout the process, stay positive and give thanks. Other things will come in the way to get you off the path; deal with it if necessary, but get right back on the path again. When you stay focused like that, life will not deny you—but only you can determine how badly you want it.

To go all in, you need to be committed. There is a fable about the eggs and bacon meal. It is said in order to enjoy an egg and bacon meal, the chicken is involved, but the pig is committed. In this case, you need to be the pig. In order to enjoy that bacon, you're going to have to make some sacrifices. You may have to give up or postpone a few things. It may be some relationships, money, or delayed gratification. Success comes with a price. If you are truly serious about succeeding, you must decide; you're either committed, or you are not. *"If you continue to do the same thing, in the same way, and expect a different result, it is called insanity."* Albert Einstein. So, decide if you only want to be involved, or be committed. However, in order to go all in, you need to be committed.

When the opportunity presents itself, seize every moment to work on your goal. Like the price on a stock chart, our energy levels has peaks and troughs; it goes up and down. Certain times of the day, you are at a highest performance level and can tackle any task, but at other times your performance may taper off, and you are not be at your peak. Some people do best early in the morning, or after breakfast. Others do better in the evening, or at night. You know yourself better than anyone. Find what those peak moments are for you, and take advantage of those times, get done as much as you are able. Whether you need to read a book, get on the phone to follow-up with clients, send out those emails, study new material, or write a speech—whatever time is your peak energy state—use it to your advantage to work on your goal.

Be Bold and Courageous

WHAT MATTERS MOST
IS HOW YOU SEE YOURSELF.

I had a friend who once used to say to me, "Let's get bold and courageous." She would say that whenever we were going to engage in something that would take us out of our comfort zone. Facing challenges is just a way of life, and we all handle it differently, whether it is starting a business, seeking to acquire a new account, going on a job interview, or whatever; it can sometimes make us uneasy and take us out of our comfort zone. The funny thing is, whenever I would tell myself that I was going to be bold and courageous, it would inspire me to take on whatever the situation I put my mind to. Just by repeating it and saying it out loud, would motive, inspire; and propel me forward to take the leap. Being bold and courageous also means to overcome your fears; you sometimes have to "JUST DO IT." - Nike.

I remember my first tennis match. I joined a team with some seasoned players. I had never played competitively and had never played doubles before. I was so inexperienced that no one wanted to team up with me to be my partner. I was also afraid that if I lost the match, I would be very embarrassed and feel foolish. I was finally put in the line-up, on the last match of the season, when the team realized that they had no chance of getting to the playoff. There are five lines to be played, and I was put at line five. I was so nervous that I could hardly make it onto the court. With knees buckling, hands sweaty, and shaking, I got my racket out. We introduced ourselves to the opponents, shook hands, and started the warm up. It was now time to play. I played so hard; I put my whole heart and mind into that match and was playing as if my life depended on it. I incorporated all the strategies I had learned during practice and hit shots. I didn't know that I was capable of hitting. All I could hear was the cheering, the chanting of my name, and the encouragement from my teammates and coach on the sideline, but I stayed courageous and focused.

After the match, we shook hands, and my opponents congratulated me on a good match. Then I shared with them that it was my first match. They not only found it hard to believe but told me I was going to become a very good player. We won convincingly by a large margin. I love tennis. After my first match, the next season I was placed in the line-up to play at a higher level; no longer was I playing the fifth position.

Even though I had proven to myself and others that I could play, and win, it still took me several seasons to overcome the tremendous amount of nervousness that I felt prior to each match. I would be physically sick to my stomach two days before the match started. Getting on the court for me was a traumatic experience; my heart would palpitate while I was walking towards the court, and my knees would be buckling and shaking out of control, but I would go anyway.

I never verbalized it or shared it with my partner. I used to wonder how my teammates could be so jolly and cheerful, eating and laughing and telling jokes right before a match, and I would be so nervous. I couldn't imagine that I would ever get to that level of relaxation. I kept wondering to myself how they could eat at a time like this, why aren't they nervous? Now, after almost 20 years, I may have a butterfly or two in my stomach now and again, but not anything compared as those earlier years. To get to my goal of becoming a better tennis player, I had to become bold and courageous and step out of my comfort zone to face my fear head-on. I felt the fear and played anyway. I gave it everything I had, so that I could move up the ladder with the team each season, winning our division and city championships and state championships for several seasons after that.

Being bold and courageous also means putting yourself on the line and defying all the odds, even when the status quo says otherwise. You can talk yourself in and out of success or failure. Your conscious mind will tell you that you're too old, too fat, or too skinny, or you don't have enough education, or you're not the right gender, etc. That type of defeatist attitude only exists for one thing, and that's to hold you back and to keep you where you are.

When I first met my friend, the one I mentioned earlier that encouraged me to be bold and courageous, we realized that we had both arrived in Georgia about the same time, but from different states. My purpose was to find a job and start a new life with my two small children and raise them in an environment with open space—a backyard where they were free to play and away from the high rise building of the busy metropolitan area in New York. My new friend's goal was to go to school and obtain a Bachelor of Science degree in one of the prominent colleges and universities in Atlanta. She had no money, or even a place to stay, but what she did have was a big goal, a small jalopy for a car, determination, and a lot of faith. She not only wanted to go to school to obtain her degree, she also wanted to stay on campus; even though she was old enough to be the mother of some of the students that she would have to share a dorm room with. Nevertheless, she applied to the school and was accepted. With no support system, other than the savings from the intermittent jobs that she had held in the months leading up to starting college, she was on her way to achieving her goal. It wasn't easy, and, at times, it seemed that things weren't going to work out, but she was determined and disciplined. She found a way to do it her way and graduated with honors. Today, she is a life coach, and a minister, to young women all over.

Never count yourself out, and don't sell yourself short. It's never too late to start again. The late, great Nelson Mandela said, *"Do not judge me by my success, but by the many times I fell down and got back up again."* Maybe you feel that you have wasted a lot of time; dare to start again, and see where it leads. Time will not wait on you; as long as there is life, there is hope. Everything that you have gone through in your lifetime has prepared you for where you are. Take the shot, and commit to staying the course until you hit your target. To reach your goal, sometimes you have to be relentless, persistent, and patient. You may get to a stage where you feel that you are helpless, or you don't know what to do next, or where to go for help. If that happens, pause, and breathe. Change the channel in your mind. Take a walk, meditate, and recite your affirmation. Remind yourself why you want this goal, and what it will do for you, as well as how it will make you feel once you've achieved it. Many times, the answer is right there; you may already have it but just need that little motivation and encouragement. That's why you need to surround yourself with like-minded individuals. This is when you need to assemble your support system and do some brainstorming.

DECLARATIONS

"I act in spite of my fear."

"I act in spite of doubt."

"I act in spite of worry."

"I act in spite of inconvenience."

"I act in spite of discomfort."

"I act when I'm not in the mood."

– T. Harv Eker

Guard Your Mind

Is watching television robbing you from your reality? Do you spend your spare time watching television, or playing video games or online games? You can't wait for the next season of TV Housewives, or whatever? These are all sources of distraction. They add no value to your life or current status. Even though they are labeled as reality, most of it is staged for the camera. A television network's objective is to get ratings and boost their bottom-line. They are meeting their goals; are you meeting yours? It's drama on top of drama, week after week. Create your own reality and excitement, with your own goal. Then, when you are asked how you are doing, or how things are going, you can tell them about your next exciting thing, even if you have to postulate until it becomes a reality in your life. Your next *episode* is: "I believe that I am now walking in favor, and my goal is already achieved." Then, act like it is already so.

Be mindful of how you are spending your time—the places you go, the shows you watch, the music you listen to, and the conversations that you engage in. All of those things have a direct impact on your way of thinking, your attitude, and your mindset. As the saying goes, *garbage in, garbage out.* Therefore, be vigilant on what you choose to let in your mind. Music can be a wonderful element. It has the ability to set the mood. As much as you are able, take control of your surroundings—what you listen to as well as what you engaging in. While some messages may be uplifting and put you in a good mood, or lift your spirit, others could depress, and leave you in a depressed frame of mind. Make a conscious effort to listen to information that shares positive messages. Some TV shows, if not positive, can have a subliminal effect on our subconscious mind. Before long, you'll find yourself singing or humming them without even thinking about the words. It goes straight into your subconscious, as well as your psyche. So, focus on music that puts you in a good mood and a happy state. Listen to messages that are uplifting and upbeat. The same goes for shows or movies. If you identify with a lot of fictional characters, as well as reality TV stars that dramatize their lives to get ratings, you won't have time to live your best life and discover who you truly are, or who you can become.

Watch your mouth; guard your mind. News reports can send your mind into a frenzy. You don't have to listen to every news report; it's mostly negative anyway. Listening to the negative news before you go to bed, and/or first thing in the morning could leave you anxious and upset without you even realizing it. Why put yourself through that, especially since there's nothing you can do about it? These news outlets are paid substantial amounts of money to get your attention. They do it by using sensationalism, dramatization, sound bites and half-truths.

My teacher, Jim Rohn, taught me a simple principle: every day, stand guard at the door of your mind, and you alone decide what thoughts and beliefs you let into your life. For they will shape whether you feel rich or poor, cursed or blessed.
– Tony Robbins

Whatever you focus on expands. So, if you desire to reach your goal, you must first see yourself getting there and having the results you expect to have. When you open yourself up that way, everything else falls into place. All the energy moves forward and goes to work to make it happen. There is a verse in the Bible that says that you shall have what you say. Start seeing the good instead of the bad, all the time. Yes, the bad things do exist, and people will say and do bad things; however, you can't control that, but you can control the way you think and the way in which you respond to it.

"Therefore, I tell you, whatever you ask in prayer, believe that you received it, and it shall be yours."
– Mark 11:24.

If you haven't yet started on your journey to your goal, or you had started and paused, start again. Start by preparing yourself for what you are about to do. You have to change your thinking in order to be ready for your new venture. It's just as if you were thinking of going on a diet. If you want your diet to be successful, you're going to have to change your eating habits. One of the first things you have to do is to prepare your body as well as your mind. You have to change your mindset. Change your thinking about food. Start flushing out *stinking thinking,* such as, "I can eat everything I want, when I want, and how much of it I want." You need to prepare your body to flush out some of that old stuff that's inside of you by doing a colon cleanse. You may need to replace your daily donut, or bagel with cream cheese, for a smoothie, containing fruits and raw vegetables, for several days. Just as you would do to cleanse your body to prepare for the new undertaking, you need to do the same in order to position yourself, by surrounding yourself with those things and individuals that are going to contribute to your goal. Having close association with individuals that don't know any more than you do, will not be of much assistance. There is a quote that says, *"You can't soar like an eagle if you hang around with turkeys."* Associate yourself with the right group of people; if you do, you will have a higher probability of achieving success and that of which you are seeking.

Another reason to be mindful of how you are spending your time is that we all have negative triggers—things in our lives that if we are not careful, will easily get us off track and be our downfall. These can be our *Achilles heel.* In Greek mythology, Achilles was said to be a Greek hero. When he was born, his mother wanted him to be protected; in other words, immortal, so that no harm would come to him. She, therefore, held him by his heel and dipped his entire body in the river; however, the area of his heel, where she held him, was not touched by the water. As a result, it was his weakness, and, ultimately, that's where he was struck and killed. During a battle an arrow lodged in his heel, and that led to his death. Know your *Achilles heel;* plan for it, and be prepared to protect it, when life starts throwing its arrows at you.

In Chapter 4, you saw how, if you commit to stepping out of your comfort zone, it can be scary, and even traumatic at first, but in the end, can be rewarding. Sometimes that's what you have to do, because, if it was that easy, everybody would do it. You have to get bold and courageous. In Chapter 5, I will discuss staying focused, and not looking to the right or to the left, so you can stay on target.

ASK YOURSELF IF WHAT YOU'RE DOING TODAY IS GETTING YOU CLOSER TO WHERE YOU WANT TO BE TOMORROW

@the.gym.mindset

Chapter 5

Stay Focused

"What you get by achieving your goals is not as important as what you become by achieving your goals."
– Zig Ziglar

To achieve greatness, you will have to put your whole self into it. One foot in and one foot out will not get you very far. You have to be committed to giving it your full and undivided attention. It's like being an Olympic athlete, going for gold; you must be focused. There is no compromise; you're either committed, or you are not. Don't let someone else receive your gold metal—go all in. Avoid distractions. Pull away from things around you that can draw your attention away from achieving your goal. Move things and objects out of sight that can distract you. Make an agenda and prioritize each step in order of importance. It is important that you check them off as you go so that you can see yourself making progress. It also gives you a sense of accomplishment. Set time limits, and then assign priority to each item. Your checklist will help to keep you on track. Things may not go exactly as you planned them; just know that you may need to adjust. However, it sets the pace for you to follow. Maintain a positive attitude, even if you get off track or fall behind. Don't beat yourself up—start over and keep on going. Use positive self-talk, such as, "This is in my control," "I will keep going, no matter what." If you want to be serious about your goals, you must be specific. You must be clear; you must be able to imagine it; you must be able to taste it and smell it— all your senses need to be involved. Be willing to stretch and even look ridiculous if necessary. If you want it badly enough, life will not deny you. So what if it doesn't go as planned. Don't give up; dig deep.

Consider the *80/20 rule,* also known as the *Pareto Principle*—the law of the vital few, or the top 20%, and the trivial many, the bottom 80%. The Italian economist and sociologist, Vilfredo Pareto, discovered this concept after studying the wealth distribution of the population of Italy. He discovered that 80% of the wealth was owned by 20% of the population. This same concept has also been applied in business, sales, and other activities like working on your goals. I sometimes find myself resisting what I need to do (my top 20%) by doing what I prefer to do (my 80%). The 80% could play a role in my overall goal; however, it's not that crucial that I get it done at that time. The top 20%, most of the time, will have some significant impact associated with it. It could be time, money, or keeping that meeting appointment.

Write the vision, make it plain, and watch it manifest in your life. Make sure that you document it. It doesn't matter your backgrounds, where you are coming from, or what your financial status. If you, have a vision, write it down, start visualizing it, then do what's necessary to get started, do the work and you will see progress, so write it down, and work it. *"Write the vision, and make it plain."* – Habakkuk 2:2 (KJV). Keep your eyes focused. Focus on what matters. Take control of your destiny; don't let anyone decide or determine in which direction your life will go. Take action, and do what you need to do in order to take control and channel your energy in the direction in which you want it to go.

Arthur Ward said, *"If you can imagine it, you can achieve it. If you can dream it, you can become it."* Don't look back; looking back could cost you valuable time, resources, and energy. Looking back could also set you back. Stay focused and head towards the finish line. There will be uncontrollable circumstances along the way, some of which will be important, and may cause you to slow down, or delay. As soon as you are able, get back up, and keep going.

Another thing that will help you to stay focused is consistency. In order to succeed and to reach your goal, you need to be consistent. No matter what your target, whether you are training for the Olympics, dieting and exercising to lose 20lbs, or saving to purchase a home, some form of consistency is necessary. You must identify and remind yourself of those things that you must do consistently, and work on them, no matter what. Consistency will help you to build patience and form good habits and the fortitude necessary for you to progress and achieve success. When you have developed good, consistent habits, and unplanned circumstances (Life) come knocking on your door, you will have the discipline to handle it and get back on track, and not lose site of the big picture.

You must be determined to succeed, in spite of obstacles, and no matter what. A strong determination, patience, and persistence, coupled with consistency and good habits, will propel you further than you thought possible. Plan for success by developing a "no excuse" attitude, because failure is not an option. No matter what is taking place, declare to yourself, "I will ensure that I do . . ." (Write down whatever the goal is for you.) Keep a checklist to ensure that you don't miss anything, because when life challenges show up and push you off the range, you will need your checklist to help you refocus on your target.

Life is challenging enough. Don't let anyone tell you who you are or let their opinion of you determine your value or success. Take control of your own future by working on developing yourself, mastering your skills, and taking your right place in society. Don't let anyone steal your joy. Some people love nothing more than to make other people's lives unhappy. If they know that there is something you don't like or something they can say that can really get under your skin, they will do it.

Be the person everyone likes to be around. Sometimes things may not be going your way. If life just sucks right now, you may be experiencing a few challenges. Don't take it out on others; find a way to deal with it by figuring out what lesson you are learning from it right now. At the start of each day, first give thanks. Then find at least one thing to be grateful for. Add humor; think of something that puts a smile on your face, or puts you in a good mood and helps you to cope. Depending on your environment or the nature of your surroundings, give out as many compliments as possible. When you do, be genuine. Don't tell someone they have pretty brown eyes if their eyes are blue. Give the gift of smiles. It's free—it doesn't cost you anything unless your face cracks when you smile.

Attitude

"The longer I live, the more I realize the impact of attitude on life. Attitude, to me, is more important than facts. It is more important than the past, than education, than money, than circumstances, than failures, than successes, than what other people think or say or do. It is more important than appearance,

giftedness or skill. It will make or break a company, a church, a home. The remarkable thing is we have a choice every day regarding the attitude we will embrace for that day. We cannot change our past. We cannot change the fact that people will act in a certain way. We cannot change the inevitable. The only thing we can do is play on the one string we have, and that is our attitude. I am convinced that life is 10% what happens to me and 90% how I react to it. And so it is with you. We are in charge of our attitudes."

– Charles Swindoll

*"Action without vision
Is only passing time,
vision without action
is merely day dreaming,
but vision with action
can change the world."*

– Nelson Mandela

Life Challenges

As long as you are breathing, and as long as you are alive, you will be tested and tried. How you choose to react to it will make all the difference. *"Life is 10 percent what happens to you and 90 percent how you react to it."* Charles Swindoll. You could go through life asking yourself, "Why me?" Or you could brace yourself. Even if you take a hit and get temporarily knocked down, get back up and refuse to stay down. There may be times when you get blind-sided by situations in life that you didn't see coming, or never thought would happen to you. When it does, don't take it personally. Stay conscientious so that you don't become so overwhelmed that you stop thinking creatively or forget how to problem solve. Take a moment, and, depending on the severity of the situation, give yourself time to come back, recharge, and then regroup. In all of this, be sure to tap into your resources—your support system—that will help you to overcome and help guide you back on your path. You can't stop situations from happening, and sometimes it may appear to be coming at you from all sides and at the most inconvenient times. Try to find the lesson from each situation. If possible, see how you can turn it around and maybe use it to your advantage to help yourself and others. Sometimes, even out of the most challenging of situations, you might find an advantage that you otherwise would not have stumbled upon, had you not faced that particular challenge. When you are faced with some life challenging situations, and you are forced to overcome, if you have determination and drive, you can get all kinds of creative ideas. Your survival instinct kicks in because you are forced to sink or swim; if you decide that you can't stay there, or else you will drown, you will paddle your way to the surface, and, instead of being rescued by a fishing boat, you will find yourself on a cruise ship. In other words, whether through your own doing or through that of others, life circumstances may slap you down— but don't stay down. There is a saying, *"When life gives you lemons, use them to make lemonade."* Many charities, foundations and organizations have been created because of some adversities that people faced.

The Serenity Prayer

God grant me the serenity
To accept the things I cannot change;
Courage to change the things I can;
And wisdom to know the difference.

Living one day at a time;
Enjoying one moment at a time;
Accepting hardships as the pathway to peace;
Taking, as He did, this sinful world
As it is, not as I would have it;
Trusting that He will make all things right
If I surrender to His Will;
So that I may be reasonably happy in this life
And supremely happy with Him
Forever and ever in the next.

Amen.

The No Excuse Zone

Create a NO EXCUSE Zone period. During that period, dismiss any thought of lagging behind, avoid procrastination, and adopt a *do it now* attitude. Stay away from things or individuals who will distract you, even just a little bit. Commit to not checking your emails or your social media sites, and don't turn on the television; even listening to certain music may trigger memories and cause you to procrastinate or slow your progress. Your *no excuse* zone is compiled with a *to-do* list. Whatever is on that to-do list, you should expect to get done that day. You should follow through to completion. Do not overload your to-do list. Each time you succeed in completing your list, you will feel a great sense of accomplishment. You will experience a rush of endorphins, you will be motivated, and you will feel a sense of happiness and sense of accomplishment. Each time you complete a to-do list on schedule, have a mini celebration. Reward yourself, because often it is something you've been putting off for one reason or another.

Google image posted by:
The Green Vale School

Take Good Care of Yourself

Love yourself. While you're on your journey, do little things that bring you pleasure and happiness. Take some time to take care of yourself. Do some things you enjoy doing. Carve out some quiet time. Pamper yourself. Take a long relaxing bath. Surround yourself with aromatic scents that stimulate your senses. When you are able, periodically schedule a full body massage. Spend a day at the spa being pampered.

Peace of mind is important and healthy, so as often as you are able, enjoy some *me-time.* Believe in yourself and have faith in your abilities. Work to develop your knowledge and skills so that you can be competent. After you have acquired the skills, take action and execute. Validate yourself; don't wait for someone else to tell you who you are. You know who you are and where you're going. Know that you deserve to be happy and successful. Wake up every day affirming that you are a child of the most High God. You are successful, and happiness belongs to you. Claim it, then do everything in your power to realize it. Go about your day affirming it and act as if it's already done. If something along the way happens to deter you, remind yourself, it's only temporary and this too shall pass. It's all part of the process, as well and it is part of the tuition you pay to get to where you need to go, so don't be sidetracked. Stay on the path.

Your health is a key factor and plays a major role in everything you do. This cannot be overemphasized. Ensure that you eat healthy by having several nutritious meals daily. You should also take care of yourself by getting enough sleep and exercise. If you don't, you won't feel good, and, if you don't feel good, you won't be your best self. Some simple form of exercise, 20 to 30 minutes several times a week, does wonders for your mind and body. It is also a great way to relieve stress. At least three to four times a week engage in some type of active movement, e.g., swimming, biking, tennis, low or high impact aerobics, etc. But do some form of activity. If you're restricted, due to illness or any form of disability, then do what you can, as much as you are able.

There are many health benefits to be gained by being active. Improvise if you aren't able to walk or jog. Do whatever you are able within your limit, but do something that will keep your blood and heart rate working and operating more efficiently— to improve your circulation. It is said that people who engage in physical exercise have a greater chance of survival after being diagnosed with cancer or after having major surgery. It increases their longevity. The many benefits of physical activity include controlling your weight and maintaining your weight. If you are currently at your determined weight, you can just burn up calories. It helps to lower blood pressure, cholesterol, the risk of stroke, diabetes, depression, cancer, arthritis, and has a host of other benefits—so keep moving! Physical exercise can improve your mood and leave you feeling happier and more energetic. Another benefit of physical exercise is that it helps you to sleep better. It also improves your sex life by enhancing arousal in both males and females. According to the Mayo Clinic study, men who exercise regularly are less likely to have problems with erectile dysfunction than men who don't exercise.

Another great health benefit is laughter. So start laughing. Laugh out loud. It's been said, *"Laughter is the best medicine."* Laughing decreases stress and makes you feel good. *"Your sense of humor is one of the most powerful tools you have to make certain that your daily mood and emotional state support good health."* – Paul E. McGhee Ph.D.

Laughing and having a sense of humor is important to feeling good. It puts you in a better mood. Laughing is infectious. Laughing can spread and become contagious, therefore, lightening up the atmosphere around you. Individuals who have a good sense of humor and engage in good laughter are less likely to feel depressed. It's been said to relieve stress and even physical pain. Laughing is a *feel-good drug.* It triggers the release of endorphins (When you exercise, your body releases chemicals called endorphins. These endorphins interact with the receptors in your brain that reduce your perception of pain. Endorphins also trigger a positive feeling in the body, similar to that of morphine.). – WebMD. So, laugh more. Laughter has physical, mental, and social benefits. It binds people together, erases anxiety, relaxes your muscles and improves moods, as well as decreasing pain or anger.

> "Laughter is the most inexpensive
> and the most effective wonder drug.
> Laughter is a universal medicine."

> – Bertrand Russell

Paul E. McGhee, PhD., proposed to do a study on the effectiveness of laughter, and its impact, to determine the various ways that your sense of humor and laughing can be one of the ways to relieve stress. For instance, you may encounter stressful situations daily in your job setting, family, health, finances, or your environment in general. In some of the studies done on prisoners of war or hostages held in captivity for long periods of time, it was found that their secret to holding on and staying encouraged, day by day, was often their sense of humor. They also found that cancer patients often reported that if they did not have a sense of humor to help them cope with all the treatment they have to go through, they wouldn't have survived the treatment, much less be able to battle the disease. They said that they didn't know what they would have done if they didn't add humor to the days that were difficult. So, the point is that if those prisoners of war, who have spent so much time under some of the most horrific conditions, and if those cancer patients who have been battling with a life-threatening disease, can use humor to get through it, no matter what stress you are coping with in your everyday situation, you, too, can certainly find a way to add humor and laugh at it.

"The important question for you is, 'Is it too late to learn to improve your sense of humor? Is it too late to begin using humor to cope better with the stress on my job? Is it too late to try to use my sense of humor to get some of the health benefits that humor offers?' The answer is no, it's never too late to start improving your humor skills, using your own present sense of humor as a starting point...." – Paul E. McGhee PhD.

We are spiritual beings, so take care of your spiritual health. Just like your body, your spirit needs to be fed daily. Faith food can be in the form of books, podcasts, tapes, videos, or any forms of media. When you feed your spirit, it helps to renew your strength and emotions. Do not discount the power of faith. When you have a strong belief system, your faith will help to lift your spirit, especially in those moments when you feel discouraged or depressed. Your faith can help push you through to overcome obstacles or barriers in your mind so that you can rise to the next level. Know that the biggest battles we face are the ones in our mind, so, just as physical exercise is good for the body, spiritual exercise is good for the mind. Each day when you rise, take a few minutes to quiet the mind. Read, or listen to your favorite scripture or inspiration. Be still for a moment, meditate on it, and let it get into your spirit. Your rest is also important. If you're continuously on the go, working hard and playing hard, your body gets tired. Not getting enough rest can cause you to experience all types of physical illnesses, as well as mental fatigue. Take time to rest. It is said that the body needs at least seven to eight hours of sleep. Sleep allows the body to rejuvenate and repair itself.

"Sleep makes you feel better, but its importance goes way beyond just boosting your mood or banishing under-eye circles. Adequate sleep is a key part of a healthy lifestyle, and can benefit your heart, weight, mind, and more." – David Rapoport, MD, director of the NYU Sleep Disorders Program.

In Chapter 5, we looked at staying focused on your goals, prioritizing, and not becoming distracted. Distraction is one of the surest ways to get off track. In addition, we also looked at taking care of yourself and being in good health so that you can be your best self while you are on your journey. You don't want your health to be an obstacle. In Chapter 6, we will see the importance forgiveness and the impact it could have on your progress.

> *Take care of yourself.*
> *Mentally, Spiritually*
> *& Physically.*
> *Surround yourself*
> *With people who*
> *take Care of*
> *you as well.*
>
> – MAMA ZERA

Chapter 6

Forgive

Be forgiving of others and yourself. *Un-forgiveness* is a prerequisite for receiving your blessing. It is so critical that it's mentioned repeatedly in the Bible. *Unforgiveness* robs you of your blessing. Matthew 6:15 *"...but if ye forgive not men their trespasses, neither will your heavenly father forgive your trespasses."* Think about that for a moment.

You can do everything it takes to succeed and to achieve your goal, yet, because of your reluctance to forgive someone, you could be holding yourself back because you are harboring hate, anger, or resentment towards someone. In other words, when you pray, saying, *"and forgive those that trespass against us,"* it is a term of condition. If you are a faith believer, when you say that prayer, you are making the agreement that you will let go of all past hurts and pain inflicted upon you by others. If you believe in The Lord's Prayer when you pray, then there is no getting around it. If you honor and keep your part of the agreement, the Lord will honor and keep His part of the agreement by forgiving and forgetting your trespasses, and never hold them against you.

Therefore, the act of forgiveness is not for the person that hurt you— it is for you. No one is perfect. Unwillingness to forgive is another form of self-imprisonment. It will not allow you to grow and expand as much as you could because you are not free. Unforgiveness takes up space in your mind. It could rob you of happiness, self-confidence, and creativity. *"Unforgiveness is like taking poison, but expect someone else to die"* (I like quote.com). To help you live a victorious life, if possible, go to your offender and let him or her know how you feel. Let them know that you have forgiven them. If they are no longer around, or they have passed on, write a letter to them expressing how you feel, and state that, although they did you wrong, you have forgiven them and hold no resentment.

For the same reason, forgive yourself. If there's something in your past that you did or should have done, and it is making you feel guilty or ashamed, let it go. You need to pray about it, ask for forgiveness, and release it. Unforgiveness and guilt of any kind are like unwanted weeds in a garden; they serve no purpose. Unforgiveness creates barriers in your subconscious. Flush out those old, tired thoughts. Tell yourself, "Enough already," and refuse to live with any disappointments, guilt, or regrets. It will keep you in bondage, and enslave you, by holding you hostage to your past. Free your mind, so that you can be more creative and productive. How meaningful or important is your goal to you? If unforgiveness is standing between you and your goal, ask yourself, "Is it worth it?" Unforgiveness can affect every area of your life. It can eat away at you like a disease; it is a silent killer. Make no mistake, when you forgive someone, you're doing it for yourself. When you forgive, you free yourself from that situation and allow your blessing to flow. No longer are you in bondage. Don't block your blessing. According to Mark 11:25, *"... and when you stand praying, forgive if you have ought against any: that your father also which is in heaven may forgive you your trespasses."* Internalizing anger, because of unforgiveness, is destructive; it can negatively affect your health, your marriage, your family, your job, and even your future. It has been said that harboring unforgiveness interferes with the recovery process of cancer patients.

Dr. Michael Barry, pastor and author of the book, The Forgiveness Project, pointed out, *"Harboring these negative emotions, this anger and hatred, creates a state of chronic anxiety."* He also stated, *"Chronic anxiety very predictably produces excess adrenaline and cortisol, which deplete the production of natural killer cells, which is your body's foot soldier in the fight against cancer."*

When you pray, ask to be forgiven by anyone you may have offended, and forgive anyone who may have hurt or offended you. Let go of old grudges so that you can move on and enjoy a life of peace, happiness, and good health. An observation was made by the Mayo Clinic staff that shows forgiveness can lead to:

- Healthy relationships
- Spiritual and psychological well-being
- Less anxiety, stress, and hostility
- Lower blood pressure
- Fewer symptoms of depression
- A stronger immune system
- Improved heart health
- Higher self-esteem

> *HOLDING A GRUDGE DOESN'T MAKE YOU STRONG; IT MAKES YOU BITTER. FORGIVING DOESN'T MAKE YOU WEAK; IT SETS YOU FREE.*
>
> *– DAVE WILLIS*

Show Love

Show love and commit to helping others as much as you are able. When you help someone else, it gives you a good feeling. Be charitable, and assist when you can. Have a heart for giving; it comes back to you in many different ways. It is always a good idea to have some form of consistent giving, perhaps something that is meaningful to you and that you are passionate about. It doesn't always have to be monetary. It could be serving in other capacities such as donating your time or talent to the growth and development of a younger or less fortunate individual, spending a few minutes talking or reading to an elderly person. The ways are endless, but do something that appeals to you and is of benefit to others.

Practice the Golden Rule. Treat others the way you want to be treated. You should let that be part of your commitment to yourself. Practice empathy, forgiveness, and charity. Do not be unkind or speak harshly against others. Those types of behaviors are not only morally wrong, they could come back to you. Therefore, act with kindness, and practice big-heartedness, even in the face of disparity. There is a saying, *"What goes around, comes around,"* so be mindful of your actions, and operate above board at all times. Be the person who, whenever your name is mentioned, even if someone doesn't like you, they know you are trustworthy and fair. Let your reputation precede you. Even when others act in ways contrary to your goals, beliefs, or principles, maintain your standard and integrity. Don't let anyone drag you down with them, and don't stoop to their level; rise above, and uphold your pride and your self-respect.

Another reason for practicing the golden rule is Karma. Karma is the Hindu and Buddhist belief that the actions of a person determine whether good or bad will return to them. Remember to acknowledge and show love and gratitude to the people that love you. Help them to understand what you are doing and why you need to do it. Let them know, in order to be successful, you need time to pursue your goal, but you love and cherish them. You don't want to achieve your big, audacious goal, and then realize that you have no one to share your success with, or celebrate your accomplishment with.

THE OPTIMIST CREED

Promise Yourself...

To be so strong that nothing can disturb
your peace of mind.
To talk health, happiness, and prosperity
to every person you meet.
To make all your friends feel that there is
something worthwhile in them.
To look at the sunny side of everything and
make your optimism come true.
To think only of the best, to work only for the best
and to expect only the best.
To be as enthusiastic about the success of others
as you are about your own.
To forget the mistakes of the past and press on
to the greater achievements of the future.
To wear a cheerful expression at all times and
give a smile to every living creature you meet.
To give so much time to improving yourself that
you have no time to criticize others.
To be too large for worry, too noble for anger,
too strong for fear, and too happy
to permit the presence of trouble.
To think well of yourself and to proclaim this fact to the
world, not in loud word, but in great deeds.
To live in the faith the whole world is on your side, so
long as you are true to the best that is in you.

Christian D. Larson 1912

Start Each day With a Grateful Heart

It's a New Day

"Today is a most uncertain day, because we have never lived it before; we will never live it again; it is the only day we have." – William Arthur Ward.

Be grateful for every new day. Each new day is an opportunity to start over. There is nothing you can do about yesterday. You can have hopes and dreams for tomorrow, but there is certainly something you can do about today. Because today is all you have, therefore, today is all you can be sure of. So live for today and do your best.

Be all that you can be right now. You may not have everything you want or thought you should have had by now, but the fact is that you are still here and that is all that matters. Don't dwell on the past or about what you have not done, or should have had by now-move forward. Maybe you missed some great opportunities. Looking back, it may be that you engaged in some behaviors that you are not so proud of now; for instance, exercising bad judgment, making bad investments, or prolonging relationships that you should have dissolved because they were toxic and did not contribute to your overall goals. You may come to the realization and acknowledgment that you have some habits that are unhealthy and are placing limits on your ability to succeed in certain areas of your life. Know this: You also have the ability to develop new habits and take action to unlearn those undesirable ones. It won't happen overnight, because they were not formed overnight; however, with the proper help, determination, and persistence, you can work to change them, one habit at a time.

Whatever the circumstances that resulted in you not being further along in life than you are right now, dismiss it, and get over it. Stop looking back—that will not serve you. Keep looking forward. Looking back is like driving but keeping your eyes focused on the rear view mirror instead of the windshield in front of you. Start where you are, and keep moving. Use past mistakes and missed opportunities to learn and to grow. Sometimes it is OK to pause and pray for wisdom and understanding. Start over and look to the future. Make today the first day of the rest of your life.

"Wisdom is the principal thing; therefore get wisdom: and with all thy getting get understanding." – Proverbs 4: (KJV)

There is no circumstance or situation too much for God to handle. It is only too much for you. So do *all* you can do, all you know how to do, then pray about it, and give the rest to Him, He will do His part, and remember, He doesn't need your help, or for you to tell Him how He should fix it.

It's a new day you've been wondering around long enough, it is time to take action and pivot. Re-invent yourself by transforming each circumstance into an opportunity so you can be your best self. Use your imagination to dream your biggest dreams to:

• Develop that new product
• Start a new business
• Attend the university of your choice
• Have that dream career
• Travel to places you want to visit
• Get the promotion you want

- Living in your dream home
- Drive the car you want to own
- And on and on

Many times your circumstances will start to change when you shift your thinking. It starts with your imagination, which causes a shift in your thinking; that thinking extends to you having a different mindset, and ultimately leads you to take action. Do not underestimate the power of your imagination. Imagination can take you places, and turn situations around you could only dream of; your imagination can cause those dreams to become reality. To really use your imagination, you have to go where your mind has never gone before; in other words, you have to be out of your mind. So from now on when someone tells you, you are out of your mind, you should take it as a compliment and thank them.

"Imagination is more important than knowledge. Knowledge is limited. Imagination encircles the world." – Albert Einsten

In Chapter 6, we discussed how unforgiveness retards your own growth and success and blocks you from experiencing your full potential. Forgiving others, as well as yourself, releases you from being burdened and frees you from bondage. So, now we move onto the final chapter. Throughout this book, we looked at developing a systematic approach to successfully getting to your goal. Now it's time to take action, step forward, and *Pull the Trigger!*

Chapter 7

Pull the Trigger

You have everything you need to succeed. Each of us is born with our own unique gifts. You have greatness in you, whether or not you realize it.

In the previous chapters, I suggested several strategies that you could consider taking that might assist you to successfully move forward in achieving your goal. Successful people take action and follow through. It doesn't matter who you know, or how much you know; if you don't take the necessary steps, and put it into action, all it is, it's just a wish. Depending on your resources, the right timing, or the right market conditions, you could take off and experience massive amounts of success, or, if you are like most people, you make a start and experience slow, steady progress if you stay consistent. It doesn't matter, as long as you are doing something and making progress. Whichever way it goes, it first requires you to take some type of action. It's not that we don't know some of these things already; it's that we don't put them into practice so that they can work in our favor for us to be successful. Therefore, the nuts and bolts of it are that you must get started and follow through till you finish, and then celebrate your win. It is not complicated, and it should be clear to you by now that you need to:

- Have a goal
- Write down the goal
- Be specific
- Have an achievable goal
- Have a sustainable goal
- Have clarity
- Set a timeline
- Keep those visual images of you achieving it at the forefront of your brain

Stop thinking about it, and just do it. *"You can't build a reputation on what you are going to do."* – Henry Ford. If you think you can, you will. Challenge yourself, and challenge your way of thinking and your self-limiting beliefs. You will find that you know more than you think you know and that you are able to do far more than you thought possible. Don't stop learning. Commit to being a lifelong learner. There is always more. As the world turns, so do we. We are always evolving. Make up your mind that you are going to start, and continue by staying focused, by being committed, determined and persistent. You are the only one that can make that decision, and, if you believe it, you will be unstoppable. Let nothing or no one, stand in the way of your success.

Be bold and courageous. Act with sincerity, honesty, and integrity in all that you do, and you will reap the benefits of success and peace of mind.

If you think you are beaten, you are;
If you think you dare not, you don't.
If you'd like to win, but you think you can't,
It is almost a cinch that you won't.
If you think you'll lose, you're lost;
For out of the world we find
Success begins with a fellow's will
It's all in the state of mind.
If you think you're outclassed, you are;
You've got to think high to rise.
You've got to be sure of yourself before
You can ever win the prize.
Life's battles don't always go
To the stronger or faster man;
But sooner or later the man who wins
Is the one who thinks he can!
– Walter D. Wintle

Don't allow your goals to be buried with you. Share them.

Defy all those people who doubted your or told you that you couldn't do it. All those that made you think that you were not good enough. Go ahead—Step out, and be bold! **PULL THE DARN TRIGGER!** DO IT NOW and CELEBRATE.

CELEBRATE WHAT YOU ACCOMPLISH, BUT RAISE THE BAR EACH TIME YOU SUCCEED.

MIA HAMM

About the Author

Una Richards is a team leader and has held a leadership role for over 30 years. She has been a manager, a mentor, and a coach to the many colleagues and staff over her long career. She obtained a Bachelor's of Psychology Degree from New York University and a Masters of Service Management Degree from Mercer University. She has discovered that by employing these seven strategic principles suggested in this book, she has successfully achieved some of her own goals. Her intention is to inspire, motivate, and encourage others to identify and remove barriers, real or perceived, that might be holding them back from achieving their goals.

073

Made in the USA
Charleston, SC
03 March 2017